WORSHIP THE PIG

Also by Gaylord Brewer

WORSHIP THE PIG

poems

GAYLORD BREWER

RED HEN PRESS | PASADENA, CA

Book layout by Talar LaSalle

Library of Congress Cataloging-in-Publication Data

Names: Brewer, Gaylord, 1965– author.
Title: Worship the pig : poems / Gaylord Brewer.
Description: First edition. | Pasadena, CA : Red Hen Press, [2020]
Identifiers: LCCN 2019049134 (print) | LCCN 2019049135 (ebook) | ISBN
    9781597098526 (trade paperback) | ISBN 9781597098076 (ebook)
Subjects: LCGFT: Poetry.
Classification: LCC PS3552.R4174 W67 2020 (print) | LCC PS3552.R4174
    (ebook) | DDC 811/.54—dc23
LC record available at https://lccn.loc.gov/2019049134
LC ebook record available at https://lccn.loc.gov/2019049135

The National Endowment for the Arts, the Los Angeles County Arts Commission,
the Ahmanson Foundation, the Dwight Stuart Youth Fund, the Max Factor Family
Foundation, the Pasadena Tournament of Roses Foundation, the Pasadena Arts &
Culture Commission and the City of Pasadena Cultural Affairs Division, the City of
Los Angeles Department of Cultural Affairs, the Audrey & Sydney Irmas Charitable
Foundation, the Kinder Morgan Foundation, the Meta & George Rosenberg
Foundation, the Allergan Foundation, the Riordan Foundation, Amazon Literary
Partnership, and the Mara W. Breech Foundation partially support Red Hen Press.

First Edition
Published by Red Hen Press
www.redhen.org

Acknowledgments

Worship the Pig is, I suppose, my Americas book. Most of these pieces were composed during three residencies: a few weeks in San Ramón, to see what my old friend Royce Slape was up to with his ODYSSEYS Costa Rica; at Alderworks, near the vanished Gold Rush town of Dyea, Alaska; and most recently at Casa Na Ilha on the Brazilian Island of Ilhabela. Yes, it's a hard life. In the last two instances, thanks to Jeff Brady and Marina Louisa Caamaño. Any remaining poems were written out at the house in Tennessee, with the usual interruptions.

Continuing gratitude and affection to Kate Gale and Mark Cull. Red Hen Press is the best friend my poetry's ever had. Just don't tell them I said so.

Thanks to the editors of the following journals:

20/20 Vision: Scotland: "Edinburgh Ekphrastic"; *Asheville Poetry Review*: "Black Sails," "Bonete Beach," "Momentary Interruption," "On a Clear, Hot Morning in Brazil, Balcony Overlooking Mountain and Sea, I Think of My Parents in Kentucky"; *Atlanta Review*: "Last Morning at the Farmers Market in San Ramón, una Oda a las Frutas"; *Birmingham Poetry Review*: "Solution to a Morning of Little Possibility: Frying Bacon"; *Briar Cliff Review*: "Hummingbird, Moonflower," "While"; *The Cape Rock*: "Crested Caracara"; *Ekphrasis*: "Edinburgh Ekphrastic"; *Descant*: "Aubade with Sunshine, Mango, and Hibiscus Following Two Days of Rain"; *El Portal*: "Para el Último Día, un Pequeño Poema de Perro para Decir Adiós"; *Evansville Review*: "God's Laser Beam!"; *Evening Street Review*: "Prayer to the Sky over Juneau Airport, Grounded for Two Days"; *Front Range Review*: "Until the Sky Quiesces"; *Kestrel*: "Merely, in an Unforeseen Moment," "When It's Done Right"; *Literary Leo* (contest winner): "Caminata por la Tarde" (as "Marcher Ruse"); *Poem*: "Asterocampa celtis," "Victory March," "Wanted"; *Potomac Review*: "Economics," "Fire on the Mountain"; *River Styx*: "Devil On a Leash"; *Skylight 47* (Ireland): "Footwear for Foreigners"; *Slippery Elm*: "October Afternoon, Witness's Account"; *Southern Poetry Review*: "Snow Day"; *Southern Review*: "Les abricots"; *Spillway*: "Author Photo, Monaco, 1984"; *South Carolina Review*: "A Little Poem to Life"; *Steam Ticket*: "Better Than Sex"; *Sugar House Review*: "Caretaker," "Late in the Narrative," and "They will mistake."

"Worship the Pig" won the poetry category of Literary LEO 2020 and was published in *Leo*'s annual supplement in the March 11, 2020 edition.

Contents

III: Wake of Vulture, Parliament of Crow

IV: Dark Bright Morning

WORSHIP THE PIG

You have to hold out for the wine, even blood, nights that are actually dark, bears that aren't teddy, gritty women like you actually know, children who die contorted into question marks, the sun on people who never bought lotion, the human voice not reduced to prattle, animals who have never been watched, the man who cuts all the ropes so he won't hang himself.

—Jim Harrison

So passeth in the passing of a day,
    Of mortall life the leafe, the bud, the flowre,
    Ne more doth flourish after first decay
    That earst was sought to decke both bed and bowre . . .

—Spenser

Man, I hit him with punches that'd bring down the walls of a city.

—Frazier, on Ali

When It's Done Right

and that happiness,
when it's done right,
is a kind of holiness . . .
　　　　—Mary Oliver

This morning you are crazy
　　in love with the heat on your legs,
　　　　sun-cure to welts on ankles—

as flies and chiggers
　　have also been lately enraged
　　　　with joy. You listen to the breeze

with a lazy rapture,
　　to the river on its cold journey.
　　　　How snow-shapes on the mountain

have changed these last weeks—
　　lunging dragon replaced
　　　　by a kitten in a necktie.

The cough of a tractor engine
　　is acceptable, as is the rooster's
　　　　mistimed reveille, even

the plaintive caw of raven.
　　No schematic for conquest,
　　　　no reckless conclusions,

no tenuous argument of connection
beyond the simple truth
of what accrues together.

A dull day ahead free
of usefulness. Say this is doing it
right, this résumé of sun,

light, breeze. Of bare legs, silted
creek, birdcall unanswered.
This singular moment

brimming with nothing special
and having happily forgotten
what you needed to say.

I

DARK HELLO

Yes I long for you
not just as a leaf for weather
or vase for hands
but with a narrow human longing . . .

—Leonard Cohen

Footwear for Foreigners

You fool. You innocent. You . . .
Southern belle. Believer in nap
on the beach and sun-dappled stroll,
in God's pure, punishing heat
and rebirth by umbrella cocktail.

Your sandals are worthless, child—
worse, an affront; worse still,
a head-shaking amusement—
relics of a people rightly extinct.
Your beloved loafers a sodden

and defeated misery. Those backless
velvet slippers, those low-cut,
sweat-resistant jogging socks?
Horsefly and mosquito greedily
accept the offering of flesh.

Kid, this is cold marsh and bad
omen country; mud-trail gurgling
muck country; bone-chill blinding
rain country; mountain knocking
you onto your soft ass country;

flood country; avalanche country;
the gold's long gone country;
should have known better country;
twenty gray hours a day to confuse
your soaked prayers country.

Summertime! The natives look you
up and down. Down, mostly—
a quizzical indictment of the feet
that somehow, from a land beyond
imagination, delivered you here.

Field Guide for the Disconsolate

Beyond gate and electric fence
the path picture-perfect, twisting
in blind bends, with sufficient rise and fall
that attention must be paid
to the challenge before you, away from
mossy crags where the beast
of your dreams will one day emerge.

The "bench" you'll discover to be
a damp plank nailed to a cottonwood stump
three spread hands wide. The cottonwood
a tree of lore, sturdy branch of preference
for hanging a man by the neck
until dead, before God and jury.

Once you clamber onto the seat,
wincing or not at the effort,
the show is all about the river: old war
of water across stone, great fist of boulder,
the frothing white split
into a thunderous division,
neither side passable, not to the adventurous,
not the plain-spoken, not the believer of signs.

Much of this doesn't matter.
Not cottonwood or wildflower,
not paralyzing fruit of the baneberry,
or, if you must, "diaphanous drape of cloud"

obscuring and revealing the mountain face.
Not any names of the moment
or tentative this or that
that flits through an overwhelmed brain.

Only the cold dark surge, parting and rejoined,
foaming, riotous, immutable, so loud
that, with practice, you disappear.

Those paying attention will recognize
our direction from the beginning:
The scale of landscape to restore your proper
size. The storm of current to deafen
your silly, gibbering mind.
Resources that remain freely available for use,
night and day.

Dark Hello

Day after day you waited,
patience strained
toward the moment
of my voice,
asked only some good news
to justify the expense,
some kindness, laughter.
You asked too much.
When I spoke
my voice was a blade
that frightened me
and your wound the reward
for your faith.
I felt your eyes lower,
your shadowed face turn
from this
harsh wrong instant
now never to be unspoken,
an echo through the air
never stilled,
a wish reborn
into a world once again
it would not survive,
world of silent
apologies for nothing
that can ever be explained.

Les abricots

Apricots on the White Summit Pass,
at the only grocer in town? Might as well
invest in that mesh of soft tangerines,
that single stone-hard pineapple, provenance

unknown. Still, they looked the part:
bright of color, firm of body, the tickling
fuzz, sexy crease. So he fell for the idea of them,
cradled a sackful back to his cabin.

The first, raised to lips between thumb
and forefinger as he surveyed a blustery
afternoon, was its own inevitability:
pithy, tasteless flesh, a mouthful of disgusting

goo spat right into the trash can. The rest
of the torn mess followed. The man
was trying, you see, for a private poignancy,
a longing or fulfillment, he wasn't sure.

Although he knew better, or apparently
didn't. Anyway, there he is in his head,
scooting along the D900 with his pretty wife,
from Avignon toward a long-awaited return

to Bonnieux and their youthful dreams—
the unseasonable heat, the unhurried hours,
the glorious golden light of the Luberon,
Jesus H.!—and why not the lavender fields,

and don't forget their goofy-tall Peugeot,
and finally the fruit stand which returns us
to our theme. He chooses late cherries,
with the seller's assistance a single peach.

But his wife all week has been about
les abricots, those sweet, glowing perfections
of which she cannot get her fill. So the apricots
of the Great North, call them a reflex,

an endearing weakness to invoke gratitude,
or regret, a conjuring taste of good fortune
or sad savor of squandered opportunity.
He wasn't sure, felt the meaning would announce

itself. As he tossed each one—plunk, plunk—
easy points in the basket—plunk, plunk—
and the Peugeot veered away in a rise of dust,
maybe it had. Lone fruit on the counter

homage to his romantic streak, or his idiocy,
or his boredom, as you please. Meanwhile,
a tease of sunlight, cold clouds settled in.
Either way, Provence was a whole different map.

Blessed Is the Lover of Animals

You never saw the bunnies discovered
between hibiscus and hollyhock,
knew from experience to give wide berth

with the garden hose. Padded by your
dog's plush fur, pine needle rising and falling
with nascent breath, the tiny beating

hearts, the small trembling bodies
growing courage every day. How darling!
So when your wife wakes you from a dream

you recognize the urgency, but, groggy,
can't quite place it. Trepidation? Fear?
There is something on the porch. I don't know

what it is. Can you come and look. Not a question.
You sit up fast, fumble for your glasses,
limp-stumble through the house toward

whatever dreadful fate. There the obscenity is
beside the Adirondacks—unspeakable, known
by instinct before brain, violation:

A mark of crimson framed, almost as if
in message, by two severed legs,
little paws clinched and luckless. In the center

between, a single organ, large as a quarter
and pale as the moon. Naked but
suddenly urgent on your knees, you lift

each sticky dismemberment, palm white
coin of, what, lung?, approach the woods
and toss it all as if in solemn ritual.

Then, still naked—for this now is the work
of the penitent, this mutilation is on you—
you fill pitcher with water and splash

bloodied wood, work stain with fingertips.
Thus the curtain of the new day riseth.
Take some good advice. Get on with brewing

coffee, with sports scores, bills to pay.
Wash your hands. For God's sake pull on
some shorts, a t-shirt, your soft slippers.

You did your thing. You did what you could.
Forget about interrogating the causes:
What if you hadn't so lovingly brushed

your dog outside each day, wind-blown tufts
a den's heavenly materials? What if
you hadn't tended the flowers with such

toil and care, until shoulders sang
a warning song of pain? What if
your nightly hymn to screech owl—

so cute, so inquisitive, so cruelly hungry—
hadn't beckoned to these woods,
enticed the monsters to the dusky edges

to note a man cooing ridiculously
to a pile of needles? What if you'd never
bought the damn house in the first place,

never indulged in bourgeois
notions, a softness that gets others killed?
Forget such foolishness. Still, in your over-

heated mind the severed legs remain,
the pale whatever absurdly large
on a dark splotch. How could that baby,

poised to emerge, have possibly contained it?
Where now the brothers and sisters,
grieving mother? Forget addled questions.

Forget green grass, blue sky. Red
is nature's color. Forget that empty hole
no longer a nest, wide and deep as your fist.

To a Dead Shrew

And if I remain a mystery to myself after so many
years, a mystery that I have known well, what of that?
Why was I even on that shadowed path at 7:00 a.m.,

beside a stream where a few late salmon struggled?
I will tell you. I had hitched a ride into town
for weekly shopping, the lone morning the grocer

restocked his shelves. A coincidence to ponder:
On the scenic drive, tired passenger veering between
mountain and estuary, I saw the first, a dark dot

racing for safety. Then town, time to kill, your still body.
Pleasant enough place for what would come. But
two shrews in a morning? One scurrying, one freshly

dead? What could it mean? And why did I know
even before deciding that I would place you in the pocket
of my coat, and that I could tell no one of this?

So I assembled a routine basket of bread and jam,
milk, juice, onions, garlic and steak, some sweets,
arranged the heavy packages so as to protect you

from their weight, and lugged all to my return ride.
Why do I tell this story, to whom and for what benefit?
Let's finish: I buried you in the garden forbidden

by ropes, beside a struggling stem of purple hyssop—
kneeling, digging fast with the spoon so not
to be exposed. The sandy earth fell away easily.

Nestled your softness into the cool hole, filled it.
I see the spot from here, past the window where I offer
this rambling account that resolves nothing, explains

nothing. I know this: Today is unreasonably warm,
glowing with sunshine. Spirits are buoyant. But
the heat will quickly do you no good, my little friend.

Slide Cemetery

After weeks of heavy snowstorms near Chilkoot
Pass, the weather shifted radically on April 2, 1898,
and warm wind began blowing from the south. Next
day—Palm Sunday—the whole mountainside roared
loose. Victims were found frozen forever in a running
position.

For some gold seekers, Slide Cemetery was
only one of several burials.

You will find it only if you seek it out,
then only by foot, horseback, or hardy bicycle
if the journey's to matter. You must exert the body.
Today Slide Cemetery is a quiet place,

perhaps more peaceful than one bargained for.
The spruce are the grandest in the region,
botanical cause of which remains a mystery.
The most astounding rise in a maze of tortured,

interlocking arms. Their effect on the visitor
requires little imagination. The giving earth
of the pathways, ferns in uncurling profusion over
decrepit plaques—themselves only rotting

facsimiles—a soothing sense of abandonment.
Oh, specifics remain, protocol of name and place—
O.W. Anderson of S.F. Cal.; S. Atkins of Baker City,
Oregon; Walter Chapper of New York, NY.

But where W. Grimes set passage no longer known,
nor what home Mrs. A.U. Maxson dreamed of.
James Edward Doran of Minnesota "Died Age 23."
James Leo is "Gone But Not Forgotten."

The most compelling constant the date of every
leaning marker. Did I mention April 3 is my birthday?
Forgive me. Crossing the mossy boundaries,
reading and rereading the date, inhaling its piney

decay, I grow preoccupied. How many died that holy
day still disputed, how many lie jumbled here.
And one born of the day to walk among them.
Slide Cemetery is a calming and solitary spot,

highly recommended whatever the date
of birth or death. Once arrived, short of breath,
strangely anxious, you will find yourself alone
with your thoughts, only a halo of flies for converse.

You've come this far. No one's watching.
Feel the rough wood against your fingertips,
the charred date—April 3—the cool
green unfurling. Listen to wind rattle the tangled

cage of tree, and through the camera's lens
detect the sphere of white lucent
through those black branches, a trick
of light undetectable to the mortal eye.

Whisper It Again

Perhaps twitchy with hunger,
peripheral, say the deer mouse who appears
for a handful of seed sprinkled
across planks to see what they would bring,
furious with her tiny hands,
big ears wide to the night approaching.
When you turn from the shadows, she is gone,
blur with a trailing tail. Look again—
she is back at work on the black shells.

Or the shepherd dog, coaxed inside,
cautious, overfilling the cabin
as she listened to disappointments,
all the woes of life, then an improvised song,
watched your back, smelled curry and sage—
until the spell ruined by one uninvited.
Perhaps tonight she returns, distanced
beyond the steps but knowing you need her,
her perfect sufficiency.

My point is, the moment that can save you,
begin to lead you back to yourself,
will answer only when you cease to ask.
Patience, humility, the luck that flashes,
sometimes, for those who listen.
Let the rest go. All that anger you earned.
The crumbs of betrayal, the narrow margin.

When the gift arrives, celebrate it
simply, without question, with gratitude and joy.
And if, say, a bonfire distracts
between trees, its human enticement,
do not approach, do not submit.
Whisper to yourself what you've learned.

Merely, in an Unforeseen Moment

In three days I begin my
journey home from the north.
No, I do not invoke the
well-worn historical hardships,
body broken on the trail,
dream reduced to a mocking
ice, reckoning of dust.
No fortune gained or lost here.
But it would be a sad thing
if the ferry cantered into
the cold blackness of the fjord,
or either plane erupted
into a miniscule comet of flame.
Or merely, in an unforeseen
moment between now
and then, I placed hand
on chest and never woke up.
Sad not to touch you
or see my home, to lose any
odds of being a different man.
No sadness to me, of course.
I would no longer exist.
And to you, sad only as a faded
cloth, a blurred face until
you also pass to a darkness
that does not remember or forget.
Thinking does no good.
I've my lucky claw, my virgin

salt, my witch's promise.
I count the hours until
I pack my bag, until the boat
motors into the dark passage,
until I take my chances.

Prayer to the Sky over Juneau Airport, Grounded for Two Days

To the timeless beauty of your fog,
the descended force

of your white silence, I lower my head
in wonder. Again, your power

humbles. But if, not even
tomorrow, but by the next morning,

perhaps around 7:10 a.m.
you might deign to lighten your mood

with a few grayish streaks of blue,
just sufficient to return to the world

the navigable reality of mountain,
directional churning of sea,

and in that window of rebirth allow
one bird, at least, clear path for its journey,

perhaps Delta #2220 for Seattle,
and get me the hell out of here on time

and in one piece, glory be
to your beneficent winds that raise

that wing! Then smother the whole
damn place for all I care. Amen.

II

OH, LUCKY MAN!

In case someday this should become
no more than an anecdote, an incident,
I will remember: I felt alive,
even if I go on denying it forever.

—Marta Pessarrodona

Caminata por la Tarde

I am lonely, lonely,
I was born to be lonely,
I am best so!
        —William Carlos Williams

I left that town behind,
its cracked and pitted streets,
its timely projects.
Left the corrugated shacks and baleful roaming
dogs. I hiked into the ring of mountains,
a discovered path
of damp, dark earth rocky and riven. I hiked into sky
of cloud and wind, taunting rain to come.
I claimed all of it. I owned all of it.
The path grew rougher,
narrower, less distinct. Maybe I worried,
more wishful imagination than anything. Did I know
where I was headed?
For divination,
I watched the avenues of leaf-cutting ants,
sure and ceaseless beneath their burdens.
They said to keep going, up through long, whispering blades
of young sugar cane.
The ridges of green hill extended,
one to the next, then ceded to gray sky roiling
with trouble. The torrent was inevitable. When it came,
it could have me.
I hoped for a circle that would

bring me back, but not too easily, not too soon. Eventually.
Otherwise, I was lost. A grand thing.
The flushed rodent, the wet, rutted soil,
the song of wind and leaf.
An unknown village in the far distance,
the spire of its small church just discernible.
The spicy, dung-like aroma inhaled, the chill air
on calves and arms. All mine, with nothing to spare
for anyone.
In a tree so invaded with bromeliads
that I could not distinguish
the leaves of the branches from
the lusty fronds and erect red flowers,
a pair of boat-billed flycatchers
alternated fluttering into their unseen nest of sticks
and a perched vigilance,
call strident and claiming and immediate.
I studied each in turn—the black and white stripes
of the head, black beak massive
in proportion, yellow breast and rufous-tinged
wings. They watched me watch.
It was a remote spot, I suppose, for their
brood, austere yet somehow abundant and manifest.
I would find my way, preferably forward,
but back as I came if necessary.
Listen, here is what I'm saying: There are as many paths home
—or wherever you find yourself today—as there are faiths

to follow them.
Your life is your own. You decide.
Ignore their noise, their scripture,
their obvious uniforms,
their bullying and stale achievements.
Your brief life is your own. Now, while the body's
still as willing and agile as it needs to be.
Now before the storm that's coming, arrives.

Invitation

I was, I admit to you,
    lying in bed sorry for myself
        and ashamed
            of the night's routine shenanigans,

empty and useless
    as a clear morning
        passed blurrily behind
            restless sheer curtains.

I would glance out, turn away,
    peek again at all that brightness
        I couldn't face. Then
            the quick dart

of a hummingbird by the rail.
    Left, right, hovering.
        There were no flowers there,
            no color, nothing

to nourish or attract.
    I reached
        for my eyeglasses, knowing
            I'd be too slow,

and pulled the curtain back.
    Ah, lovely little fellow.
        It held there, inches away,
            examining me,

my tired nakedness,
  and giving up a good look
    in return.
      The curved black beak,

gleaming lime breast,
  glossy wine-colored tail feathers
    spread in a flourish.
      That tiny heart's pulse

1,200 times per minute,
  four breaths and seventy
    furious wing beats per second.
      Imagine such

insouciance
  for life, such astonishing energy
    expended without doubt.
      The endless thirst

for sweet nectar!
  I know how absurd,
    how vain you think me
      to believe the small one

had come to encourage,
  to remind of the gift
    of this brief, radiant morning
      and gently admonish.

What's the problem now,
    Gaylord? Get over yourself!
        Let's go! It went.
            But why else? And why not

believe, accept,
    and be grateful?
        I was smiling, on my feet,
            offered the world again.

Fire on the Mountain

Who lit the blaze, for what harsh
    purpose? Smoke a ghostly breath
    exhaled across the sugar cane,

snuffing each blade. Smoke
    in smothering tendrils into the trees.
    Then the clouds, dark army,

descending. Clash or caress,
    and some acrid and shifting
    new creature born. Smoke, cloud,

the world one believed one knew
    dissolves to gray, to nothing.
    The black vultures circling,

white tips of their great wings
    reaching for it, slicing through.
    A score of others heavy

on branches, sullen, shivering.
    What would death reward them?
    And the solitary short-tailed hawk,

perched and abiding in its hunger,
    wide breast rising, falling? In
    the mist, the merciless head turns.

Crested Caracara

My God, you groan, another
　　bird poem. But wait.
　　　　What caused me to pause

on my path and turn?
　　There bending the highest
　　　　branch on the tallest

and most remote Spanish cedar,
　　with the afternoon sky
　　　　a sudden advancing black,

a sharp hungry line
　　consuming the verdant
　　　　ridgeline of the mountains,

the scattered villages,
　　in full relaxed view,
　　　　the signature black crest

like a flattop haircut
　　on the white head,
　　　　the orange cere and legs

unmistakable
　　ornaments of predation
　　　　and the day become darkness

all around, very much
as if it owned the kingdom
of its surveying,

the caracara perched, unmoving.
Do you see? This was
not the zoo of last week,

my friend, this was the raptor
arrogant, unshackled,
with only us for witness.

A Little Poem to Life

Specifically, a little night poem,
    as perhaps you pause on the balcony,
round moon teasing
    behind drifting silks of clouds
and then fully revealed to you,
    milky and luminous eye.

Perhaps you indulge the conceit
    of the moon as your fairest lover
—what harm done?—
    as in the north lightning flares
a black ridge of mountain.
    After all, you're probably a bit tired

from your exertions in the forest,
    a bit drunk and full from a good dinner.
Somewhere in the darkness,
    perhaps you recall the playwright who
hanged herself at twenty-five, the summer
    of her last year when she refused

to meet you in London.
    Perhaps—anything is possible—
that is two decades past, a generation,
    and you sit now in the sovereign
night twice her age
    that last haunted hour.

Perhaps, if you're like me, you're
    shocked at yourself that another
twenty years or so sound desirable
    —hell, make it another half century,
bartender!—inside the fading miracle
    of the body, your hands

and eyes and mouth, lunar
    mistress flirting from her veils,
rapt audience to skies split with fire,
    selfish to know just how a few
stories turn out. What fun.
    S., you're missing the whole show.

Economics

Yes, I have taken what I wanted
from this country. The trill of the thrush,
the purring of the dove. Taken
the weary grid of the city,
taken the bread of my host,
the nights and the torrents of rain.
But I have given my currency, my custom,
my sweat to an unmapped trail.
Given my blood to the flies
and my pledge to a deaf and muted deity.

What I have taken I took fiercely,
without apology, and I defy you
to condemn me for what I have done.

Late in the Narrative

The houses risen
from rubble generations
ago, solid stone
and good roofs. The road

widened and paved.
The war ended for a lifetime,
villain vanquished
in body, if not memory.

Ages since, lovers met
and parted, or met
and remained.
The old man's dead,

slumped over his plow,
and the cattle auctioned.
The children gone,
too, grown now

and happily escaped
to the city and its sequels.
The view's still nice,
but you're thirty years

too late, or maybe a thousand,
depending on the edit.
Anyway, face history—
you're a bit part,

on the end of the couch,
in the shade of the chapel,
a clever, irrelevant
remark here or there,

a minor scene or two
unlikely to survive revision.

Milking

Moments later, I would step away
　　from the shed
and witness a white hawk in flight
　　above the canopy of cloud forest,

its soaring purity
　　expanded to black wingtips.
But before the divine, the comic.
　　Hunkered on a stool,

another novice too gentle
　　with the formidable, rubbery lobe.
Squeeze, twist, tug. Dribble.
　　She didn't care. The feed in the trough

was feed. Jorge talked me through
　　again: mammary firm between
thumb and index, forefinger
　　for support—twist, squeeze, hard pull.

A steady stream sizzled into the pail!
　　When I fed the calf,
she greedily sucked a half gallon,
　　plastic nipple locked in place

until the bottle was finished.
　　My mouth watered. With permission,
I milked a glassful. It took a while.
　　The frothing white line slowly rose.

Then I stood, and drank,
    the sweet rich cream
warm over my tongue, down my throat,
    raw and shocking and delicious.

Jorge asked if I'd like another—
    no shortage in the taut udder.
I smiled, nodded, and sat back down
    on my stool at the bar.

*Para el Último Día, un Pequeño
Poema de Perro para Decir Adiós*

Appropriately, a Sunday
    and the trees and metal roofs
    glow under the bright

morning sky. The dogs
    have escaped from their enclosure—
    patio of orchid, heart-shaped

anthurium, and broad ferns,
    but nonetheless a bolted, four-walled
    world to pass the week's

minutes, hours, days whining
    and defecating. Now Cosita—
    "little thing" the larger of the pair—

out the gate into the street!
    She jogs, returns, shakes floppy
    hound ears, stretches long

on the shaded sidewalk. Kinky-haired
    Dixy, whom I have nicknamed
    "little stinky" for excellent reason,

remains inside the front bars
    of the *casa* but seems pleased enough
    taking in a sun cure,

tiny tongue lolling over whiskers,
        head rotating to the action.
        Pleased enough to roll

onto her back and offer up the small,
        aromatic belly for a rub.
        One good moment lived at a time

all there is. Meanwhile,
        four dog treats remain
        in the bag, my careful math

of two tonight, two early tomorrow.
        When I will rise, fly north for hours,
        and in the evening—God willing,

if my fortune holds—
        what a greeting receive
        at my own door, what a bellowing,

what a circling romp and attack
        of claws and kisses! Oh, lucky man!

Last Morning at the Farmers Market
in San Ramón, *una Oda a las Frutas*

Adiós to the buttery indulgence of the *aguacate*,
    the sweet milk of the *coco* mined from its hairy shell,
adiós moreover to the sultry curves of *papaya*,
    golden star of *carambola*, to everywhere tables heavy

with sharp-bladed *piña*, bright globe of *mango*.
    Adiós to the crisp tartness and rough complexion
of the *castagña*, puckering argument of forceful *limón*,
    sweet slick gelatin of the *rambutan* undressed

from its spiky armor. We walk the aisles among you,
    we devour you with our mouths and eyes,
laden stalks of fat *plátanos maduro y verde*
    in hugging rows, and not at all to forget

the stubby-thorned *guanábana*, enormous, impressive
    in its deformity, but inside above the heart
the unmarked white flesh and glossy necklaces of seed,
    nor overlook the curling fingers of *guaba*,

pulpy coolness sucked from each violated pod.
    Tart wild *moras* in season, cures of *cúrcuma* root,
and oh, on and on, countless more, names unknown,
    row upon row of earth's dowry on display,

parading amazed and heartbroken among you
    a last time, your plenitude, boundless rich reward
of sun, branch, and flower, touching you, opening you,
    taking you on the tongue, in love, in parting, goodbye.

III

WAKE OF VULTURE, PARLIAMENT OF CROW

Time passes, and little by little everything that we have spoken in falsehood becomes true.

—Proust

Wanted

You wanted the silent mornings,
disturbed only by banal prophecy
of a single bird unanswered.
Wanted to wind the clock
to your own body, rising
in slow and guiltless rhythm.
Wanted no human voice opening
into song in a farther room,
no weight of footsteps, no clang
of cabinet, plate or knife. No radio static.
Wanted the wake of each dim room,
a laying of hands on
the cool surface of bureau,
table, windowsill, chest of memory.
Wanted to breathe the early
shadows, privy to your own thoughts,
council only to the man,
better or worse, you've become.
Wanted to survey what was lost,
what might remain, consider if the future
was as gray as forecast. You wanted
what you wanted, nothing more
and probably nothing less,
to separate once again want from need.
That is, to indulge, to ponder,
to test a proof unprovable.
To listen unspeaking
until the voice you heard wanted

it all back, everything, every shout,
song and crashing door, every so-called
distraction so carefully discarded.

Until the Sky Quiesces

Lie there as long as you will
attentive to rain tattooing the deck,
one plaintive jay,

deliberate human breath.
Your chest beneath locked hands
fills with the hollowness

of recent losses, chosen and not,
of interest to no one.
Lie there, listen to the voices

and fail again to think it through.
Lie until the sky quiesces,
perhaps a more melodic

birdsong intervenes, a metronymic
drip of gutter. Either way
you'll have to rise up, pal,

each shuffling step assuming
the catalog of another day—
fat rabbit stretched on haunches

toward breakfast of privet,
mother chickadee a dart out and in
her nesting box, first

two lilies of the year, tattered flags
of gold. And the grass,
oh yes, flaming, fiercely green

on both sides of the fence.
See, your luck's turning already—
one way, then the other.

Solution to a Morning of Little Possibility: Frying Bacon

Get the big skillet from its hook,
peel off one unguent strip at a time,
butchered and cured
down the road by some old boys
who worship the pig,
and load that thing up
over medium-high heat.
Get your hands greasy, deep
in the pores, stand over it
working the rhythms until
your glasses steam,
your tongue's wagging in a wet mouth.
Let it splatter. Let it burn,
stain, and make an ungodly mess.
Forget about the menu.
Bacon takes care of bacon,
the unctuous agency of pork,
the holy salt-flesh and sweet-fat
better than Jesus
and Elvis rolled together.
Get the whole house smelling good,
the dog on high alert.
Damn it, son. This may be
the best day of your wasted life.

Apology to Constantin Brâncuși

> Work like a slave, command like a king,
> create like a god.

I'm sorry to disappoint, but it's a Tuesday,
    for God's sake, and when I give the dog a command
she stares at me sadly, and the coffee's cold,
        although the mug curves in a graceful geometry.

I've no answer this afternoon for your dark gaze
    from 1922, at the height of your powers.
We're primitive around here, but not too exotic,
        and I'm rusty on my Byzantine traditions

and Romanian peasant crafts. I can create
    another pot, if it pleases. I've never fashioned
a violin from discarded wood, but I grind the beans
        myself. I sleep an obscene number

of hours—*Sleeping Muse*—and waken slowly
    to rain and birdsong—the single quill of *Bird in Space*.
Get it? Living embodiment of your brilliance
        without even trying. You expect a lot, graybeard.

Might I remind of your remark upon
    leaving Rodin's studio after only two months?
Nothing may grow under big trees. We've many
        trees here, a boatload of shade. I believe, though,

in your later years you'd have forgiven me.
    Puttering in your white pajamas and yellow
gnome's cap, in your simple studio of hand-hewn
        furniture, only fifteen sculptures during

your last twenty years. That's *my* Constantin, the man
    I revere and love. Oh Patriarch, alone in your
silent menagerie of birds and fishes, heads
        and columns, asking yourself why all the bother.

Then a hole in Montparnasse between the others.

God's Laser Beam!

writes the first poet on the scene,
heart kicking as if he'd struck gold.
From a red seam in clouds,
a cylinder of light sweeps the contour
of the mountain. *To illumine*

our last untrammeled vein of the wild!
he adds, a bit lamely. Word out,
the poets stake claims across the balcony,
spill out into the courtyard.
A fiery scar in the eye of heaven!

scribbles one. *Search party for the dead!*
types another. Meanwhile, the painters
secure easels, sketch furiously
against time. Digital composers play
with angle, exposure. *Out of the way,*

asshole! someone yells, *The souls of the lost*
are returning for their names!
But already the column narrows,
tour of ridgeline complete.
It pales, disappears back to gray.

Thus is the sublime forever blinded!
offers a woman with a fountain pen,
perhaps superfluously.
The old man of the village pays
little attention to the artists.

They're mostly harmless. He glances
at the horizon as a red line fades.
Pretty, he thinks. There's hay to cut,
wood to haul, tillage. Always
work to do. We needed that rain.

Devil on a Leash

He's pissing blue steam
and shitting Chinese bottle rockets
when I knot the leather
in a fist and reign him in.

He claws mud and spews.
But I know the Old Boy likes it,
is pleased I caught him napping
in the thorns. He'd counted me out

of the game, a flatline of disappointment.
Plus, a little forced submission
is always nice. We reach the edge
of desiccated acres and I slip

the plow over stubby horns,
wrench it tight to the bony black back.
This maize is thine, these rows
I tithe to thee. But the initials we dig,

oh Grand Beast, oh Great Bitch,
they are mine. I boot him hard.
The hairy xylophone of ribcage
sings. Back to heaven. Back to work.

Victory March

The last animals had been salted
over flame. We had fired the last bullets
into the bodies and minds of our enemy.
It didn't matter. The city was ours.
As we marched, hollow firearms flapped
on our belts. I thought, foolishly,
of Giacometti pursued by the Fascists,
his sculptures, thin as rifle barrels,
cast small to travel in the pockets of his coat.
Our guns were no work of genius.
The handle's heft served well as a bludgeon.
It didn't matter. No weapon needed now,
for the city was ours, liberated
from those who had sought to take it.
We marched through that silence and dust,
cheered by ghost-windows, the drum
of our boots on the broken street.

Author Photo, Monaco, 1984

First the Italian ensemble, oh my:
white dress shirt with short sleeves rolled,
skinny leather tie, skinnier belt,
pleated silver slacks 30" at the waist

and of a shimmering material.
Kindly, the photographer has amputated
the white-accented wingtips of memory.
And oh, lad, that bouffant!

I was old enough by months to enter.
Now posed at the casino's elaborate doors,
leg cocked, one coolly raised hand
—roulette, random number—

fanning 200-plus dollars worth of francs.
Black and white exposure
of a nostalgia piece: "Cocky Young Asshole
Who Thinks It's All Such a Laugh."

Open-mouth smile, eyebrows raised
for the lens and the immortal future.
But here is the thing: What steals
the shot is the old man, slightly behind me,

who has paused from entering
and turned back in profile.
Belt cinched high around his squat shape,
black wristwatch above a hand curled

like a claw on baggy trousers,
gray cigarette angled in the mouth.
The toadlike head crooked in my direction—
not admonishment, not dismissal,

just a weary surveying. Sixty or more years
of the wheel's ruthless spin in his eyes.
I couldn't see him over my shoulder, not then,
both of us caught in the flash.

The Work

It's always on your own, no theory, no choice,
no skillset but necessity. Always the crew a no-show
after guarantees—not a word, not a kiss my ass.

Always the wrong tools for the wrong
job, worn blade, crowbar, bag of bolts and screws.
No "demolition hammers" here, no "sabre saws,"
no goggles and gloves and pussy nonsense.

Always one rung short, ladder overextended,
always the body contorted, juggling in space,
clown suit of stained t-shirt, torn pants, cap blued
from bleach, a blinding back-spray to paint the face.
Always the slick roof and the spot
too far for the brush, no insurance, ever,
and having to reach that spot somehow regardless.

Always the mumbled incantations
of the tribe for failed solace, ruined strength,
homage—soffit, fascia, eave, bargeboard and flashing.

And, always, the twists of wind when
still day needed, rain when clear sky promised,
punishing sun when instructions read cool shade.

Always doing it again against the calendar
of decay, the race against the flaking and the rot,
the crack, the break, the blood, always a year older,
stiffer, slower, and the end of each done day—

always behind, the fuck-up you didn't see coming
and the extra cost you can't afford—
loosening a bootlace, loosening another,
trembling to free yourself just like the old man did.
Always the work and what it gets you, what it got him.

October Afternoon, Witness's Account

At the creek earlier, dog Lucy smiling,
we flushed a hawk from shadows,
wings flashing white and auburn through the trees.

In my soft chair I considered the day's news,
the sad and violent stories,
ate without apology the last slice of strawberry cake.

The storm that floods and splinters the coast
delivers to us a cooling wind, relief
from unseasonal heat, but not the rain we need.

The last hummingbird has departed, possibly
yesterday, possibly the day before,
left its globe of nectar to implacable wasps.

Soon—though granted, this is speculation—
the house will fill with the aromas of lamb stew,
a browning loaf of rosemary bread.

Tomorrow is Lucy's birthday, my lovely girl
an impossible eight years, and, perhaps,
we will drive to the battlefield,

pursue a path among the limestone outcroppings
where their canons could not
advance. Perhaps. Everything else,

however—this clear autumn light,
the shortening hours, my sentry heart still at work—
I'll swear to it all, every last word.

Asterocampa celtis,

to the geek, to the rest of us
the hackberry emperor,
small brush-footed butterflies
clustered this morning
in the ridges of the porch stone.
You count five, six, eight
as they show themselves.
Perhaps the rock's moisture
attracts, or the garden's
fresh spread of pine needle.
Your science is dodgy,
but you smile to watch
the orange-brown wings
spread and close in unison,
the patient probing
of white-knobbed antennae,
no translation necessary.
Tomorrow, as suddenly,
they will be gone, scattered
perhaps to the rough-barked
trees of their namesake.
For now, they lighten the load
of failure. You needn't
ask why. You needn't explain.
Not why one inspects
the rawhide lace of your slipper.
Not even at what signal
they rise in a darting flurry

to hands, to the damp neck
of shirt, to your amazed
face, flinching at the touch.

While

she dreams of being roughed by a wave
onto the splintered shore of a cursed island

and he dreams of a rich holiday
where the tendrils of the grapes are vipers

while she dreams of a house consumed
by fire from a single candle lit for romance

and he dreams of a fevered terminal,
the bus to take him home that never arrives

while she dreams of ladders, he a path of stone
she of ravens, he a barred gate in the sky

while she reaches for proof of his arm
and he lays his hand on hers in confirmation

both atop the raft of their bed, too weary
to navigate further the tides of night

and the dog between them twitches, moans,
her fate of which she too cannot speak

Snow Day

Get this: First day of the semester!
The covering we've wanted for a month
arrived in the night, relieving us
our careful agenda, outline of rules.
How absurd! How fine! We hike
the creek with white dog Lucy, snout-deep
and ecstatic in the cold fluff. No tracks
but ours, human or otherwise.
Back at the house, cardinals assemble
before I can get the feeder refilled.
Racket of a red-bellied woodpecker.
I dust off the vitamin block for the deer.
There's a party going on!
It's boots puddled in the doorway,
butter cookies, a steaming mug of mint tea,
that spy novel all morning long.
When I look out to survey the wildlife,
the prints from our walk are gone.
Today's literary theme, erased identity.
Today's discourse, the *chuck-chuck-chuck*
of the red-belly. Today's assignment,
a pot of soup from whatever looks good.
Snow still coming, soft and slow.

Sunday Afternoon, Game Day

Cars suddenly nose-to-tail along
this quiet street confuse me, then I recall
the corner cemetery, long engulfed
by subdivision, and see the lingering

mourners, their requiem finished.
A black woman in black dress and hat
leans into a man's chest, a wedge of light
between them. I'd no idea

the old grounds were still in use,
that any plot remained among the crowd
of stones. Further, a wake of vultures
mount a doe's carcass in the culvert

of someone's neat front yard. Further still,
more birds rip at something smaller.
Returning soon from the grocer,
trunk heavy with fried chicken and biscuits,

soda, slaw, and gravy for our celebration,
our assured victory, convertible
open to a fine unseasonable day,
I find the vultures still at the work

of their hunger. The cars meanwhile
departed, all save one, and the tent
dismantled. A trailer tilted with soil.
Over the filled hole, two shoveled men.

The older tamping loose earth
hard with his boot. The younger also
leaping and landing—but smiling, rocking
his head in the throes of his dance.

Deadheading

More task than skill,
although of dexterous wrist
and precise motion.

Aesthetics are not involved,
nor considerations of beauty's
fleeting nature.

This is not the moment
to judge brashness
or subtlety of color, frill

of petal, droop of laden stamen,
call girls versus coquettes,
but the moment—sun hot,

sweat on your brow,
feet precise in needles
of pine—to get the job done.

The rotted mess of each
of yesterday's wonders,
quick snap between thumb

and finger, a wet thud
in a bucket. Wary, always,
of the tragedy of a bud broken,

or—carelessness with no
recovery—an entire
unbloomed scape. Not

glamorous work, watched over
by beetle and grasshopper,
disinterested robin.

But as you progress,
bent in your practiced
caretaking to separate the dead

from living, sure enough
the panorama of the new day
reveals its glorious yield.

Finish what you started—
dump the bodies in the woods,
wipe your stained hands.

Better Than Sex

Well, who's to say
really and who cares—
this is one
ecstatic bumblebee!

Drunk with love
on the slender, glowing
petals of Hudson Valley,
hind legs forcing

her deeper,
deeper, crazily deep down
the supple throat,
only a twitching

tail visible, vulnerable,
given over
and overwhelmed
and who cares

about the hive's desire,
the queen or sister
or banished male,
everything from antenna

to tarsus
a hot mess of that magic
yellow dust.
Sweet god of blooms!

She's out of her mind,
dizzy, wanton.
It's on to Golden Prize,
then Fair Annett

and reckless again down
the throat,
black legs pumping,
stamen trembling.

She wants it all over her!

Edinburgh Ekphrastic

—after a photograph by Terry Price

Note the women parading
singly up Princes Street
past the Old Waverley Hotel,

in proud service since 1848.
Note, centering the moment,
largely unremarked,

the bagpiping young busker
in full regalia of tartan kilt,
sporran, wool glengarry.

Note cheeks full on the blowpipe,
fingertips of both hands
delicate on the chanter.

Note the woman turned away,
framing photos of the sky.
Only the anonymous hiker

in the foreground, unbalancing
the composition, stares
steady on into the song.

Note, finally, the iron fence,
the severe finials of its pickets,
and behind, out of frame,

the public gardens where
each midday I would unwrap
the simple meal prepared for me,

young man in a city I loved.
"Scotland the Brave." William
Wallace. The blood roused.

Sir Barleycorn, of course.
50p flipped into the case and
on your way. So many years.

1956–2018

When the phone buzzed on the quilt
of the king-size bed to announce
the death, we were up already enjoying the sun—
punishing in another hour—

risen over the marsh, the gurgle of receded tide.
A raccoon, enormous, blackened with mud,
crossing labyrinth of sludge
into the tall blades. A painted bunting—

a male, the one you want—anxious at the feeder.
That was before the phone's headline,
those six terse words, in turn, before
our B&B's breakfast of eggs Benedict

and squeezed juice, dark coffee, seasonal melon
and berries and much smallish talk
of the day arrived and what it might offer.
For us, a pod of dolphins at the pier,

their joyous formations, but also the thing hauled
on the hook—shark or ray or something else—
left wheezing to die, bulbous eye frantic
and confused. The urgent lovemaking

of afternoon, the bathing, wine, good novel,
ritual hour on the breezing balcony.
At the restaurant, sweet local shrimps
sticky and hot on our fingers.

And six words receded but palpable on the hours.
More words had joined them, from many
halting voices. Tomorrow we were going home,
a long day on the road, God willing

without mishap. In the night, a distant storm
of lightning, far enough to be beautiful.
As my wife slept, I counted the seconds
between explosions, until the show was over.

IV

DARK BRIGHT MORNING

My story is of a calm darkness, of the root asleep
in its strength, of the smell which has no scent.

—Clarice Lispector

Worship the Pig

Holy loin, blesséd shoulder,
belly, fatback, cutlet. Sacrament
of rib, ham, jowl, and hock.
Snout to tail, border to border,

sing loud of headcheese,
pickled foot, crispy ear,
of pancetta, lardo, prosciutto.
Of sausage and casing.

Holy phrases. Denomination
of Bacon, Order of the Rump,
Sect of the Crown Rib,
Deep Cult of the Crackling.

All praise be thy earthly flesh,
thy sweet white fat, well-salted,
prepared for our good
and greasy consumption.

Turned on spit for the faithful.
Buried in a hot, covered grave.
Tended by priestly ritual
in a pit of smoking embers.

Pig oink. Split belly with blade,
pig squeal. Sever head, pig die.
We love the blood, bone,
blackened skin. Love the pig.

We dance, we pray, we dig in.
Bowed at table, we raise
the wondrous flesh to lips.
Eat in thanks, pig hallelujah.

They will mistake

your patience for indignation,
your diplomacy for
arrogance, your tolerance
for a clear disdain.
It has always been so.
Why must you behave as you do,
surrounded on all sides
by such beauty? will be
their common accusation.
Listen to me, brother.
Keep your own council
and keep it close.
Soon they will stay clear of you
and look away. This is your victory.
Obviousness is the curse.
Banality, the sin that cannot
be forgiven.
Their uneasiness,
their laughter, their joined forces.
Their beauty too easily adorned.
These are the sure signs.
The day, brother, is for vigilance.
Guard yourself. I will
no longer be here to assure you.
Listen to your heart
and breath. Otherwise, trust
silence. Be patient
of what has been nurtured

from the beginning.
Later, the house overtaken
by shadow, hold congress
with the night heron,
the banded owl, the dark beauty
of a song the others
will never know.
You will be magnificent.
And I will meet you there.

Only Human

The fine day forecasted arrives,
day intended for a hike south
up coastline, away from weekend bustle,
keep company with tern and gull,

toe the small dead crabs on hard sand
and indulge your trademark solitude.
Confess it: There is something
about a Sunday, July sun high and hot,

distant radio playing a song you've
never heard, that beckons instead
to the village, right into the dangerous
thick of the hive. To the dingy fishing pier

where dark, quiet men congregate
to smoke and a single dim counter
offers the sea's morning wares.
To the public square, the Church of

Our Lady of What the Hell bright above.
Below, industrial Christ on His cross,
savior of stainless steel and rusted springs
passed by all without notice.

To the narrow beaches, the *commedia*
of flesh—good, bad, indifferent,
well-inked, bulging or withered, impossibly
young or aged. And how do you grade

yourself these days? Week complete,
who may judge if one joins the promenade?
Take solace that language
will keep you isolate, a gauntlet

of babel through which you pass,
untouched, among but not of the crowd.
For interaction, the pidgin verse
of commerce: from the grocer, provision

of red wine and, if any remain,
her soft rolls smelling of yeast.
From the druggist, lotion against
the treacherous, invisible *borrachudos*

that make the holy day complete.
So go now, retrieve your hat and coin,
your cloth bag to fill. Get moving.
It's Sunday, and you're only human once.

Caretaker

Here is your bread, sweetened with honey
as preferred, here your portion of milk,
thick with cream and cold. Here your chair,
placed just so before the small desk, before
the window I have opened wide onto the world.
Whether this new day offers flower
or sword, lyric of praise or bitter lament,
a palette of holy light or a bruised darkness,
grace or sorrow, the sparrow or the snake,
whether the boat powering for the sea
rushes lonely from a failed life or hurries
joyous toward reunion, is not for me to know.
Here, the breeze to cool your brow as you
name truth from falsehood. Work complete,
here a round of aromatic soap, soft towel
to cleanse and dry the body, this sheet
stiffened in the sun I have tucked and smoothed
for your dreams. That you may discover
the phrase, the form, the hue of your longing,
I have offered my simple attentions. Take them
with pleasure. Whether my service had
meaning or was a wasted life, is in your care.

Aftermath

Rise, poor Lazarus. How long do you
intend to bear your hard, disheveled bed,
the wind's sighs of disappointment?

You've arrived again, where you swore
never to return. Get on your feet.
Take a token stare in the mirror, or not.

The door rumbles at your approach.
But no one lurks beneath the stair
with stones and accusations. The red brush

still blocks your passage in its profusion,
still maddens bird and wasp
that couldn't care less of purported sin.

See, no hangman hovers in the kitchen
with black hood to smother you,
just coffee already brewed, a guileless

hello, the workers out in the sun
busy at their hammering. Perhaps
a young woman smiles from the hallway,

says she approves of your silly shirt.
Or the host appears, inquires without
suspicion of your day's agenda. That simply,

the rickety wheel of consequence creaks on,
greater than one soul's foolishness.
You've risen again from the dead,

learned again the world's indifference
is no different from its pardon.
That this is a continual blessing.

On a Clear, Hot Morning in Brazil, Balcony Overlooking Mountain and Sea, I Think of My Parents in Kentucky

Earlier there, they stir from their restless sleep,
by drowsy increment choose to get up and face facts.
First the bathroom necessities, the weak coffee
gurgling toward the pot. They will then gather
from separate beds to speak of this and that—
the night's dream or memory, an unexplained sound,
their youngest son's unending restlessness—
and make their first adjustments to the day's pain.
My father's twisted wrists and deafness, his recent
shuffling frailty still startling to witness.
My mother's swollen ankles, her cold that won't leave,
the lingering disappointment, worsened by everyone
thinking her a fool, that she did not win
the sweepstakes they promised—that morning
she set the alarm, did her hair, and nobody came.
Why am I telling you all of this, these intimacies
that break my heart and have broken theirs,
this sadness shading every gesture, that turns
paradise into a senseless rebuke? Listen, this poem
is none of your goddamn business. Nor the paltry
options of the day ahead. Forget joy. How about
any distraction to kill an hour, to hold back the walls?
Dad's solitaire at the kitchen island, an afternoon
drive to the grocery to hunt expired bargains.
Mom's visit to a backyard grave, quick cry
and a name invoked before the July heat locks inside
all but the foolhardy. First, time for the ordeal
of breakfast, weary choice of fried or scrambled,

exhaustion of jam and of toast to butter,
counting pills—just getting all the shit on the table.
I don't want you knowing any of it, or your opinion,
least of all your sympathy concerning lately visits,
a nearly unbearable cocktail of helplessness,
frustration, guilt—take your pick, but don't.
The oldest story in the world, and the most banal?
Sure. Until it's yours, these two you love dearly,
sixty-five years together with hardly a night apart,
whom you miss already as they leave you step by step.
We'll see how tough you are, when the time comes.

Aubade with Sunshine, Mango, and Hibiscus
Following Two Days of Storm

Wash of light across decking.
On your cheek, exquisite heat. You turn
toward it, a plant soothed and nourished.
Yesterday beneath the bruised sky
you ate the best mango of your life.
Fleshy, bursting orange, dripping and sweet.

Hunched, gnawing the skin,
mess of chin and hands, syrup pooling
between knees. Two last slices
offered to the night. This morning, yes,
your evidence of beak or claw. Two days.
The storm and what it carried.

Now the hummingbird hovers at an obscene
stamen of hibiscus flower, squeaks,
lands compactly on a branch. Nothing stays.
Only the fool speaks any more of redemption.
But in this fleeting instant that lasts
forever, you sit still, face to the sun,

warm, breathing, and nearly forgiven.

Note Unsent

For reasons unclear
I think of you,
wish you to see this place
of beauty.
The quick math
astounds:
a decade passed. It seems
unimaginable.
That we have not
spoken saddens
but does not
surprise.
We could sit quietly
on the balcony, courteous
of how time
has marked us.
The sunsets here
are brilliant, blinding.
By ritual
I stare into
that circle of fire.
They happen
quickly, require timing
and attention,
a delicate
understanding.
I believe that you would
come to
cherish them
just as I have.

"Limoney"

A man climbs a path to investigate
a blue and white chapel facing the sea.
He finds a locked gate, parade of holy
figurines, peeling paint and plaster.

Slim clues to the mystery of its origin.
A stormy death? An awaited return?
Oh well. The stones jut forward, offering
new perspectives. From where he sits

the man can see the next curving beach,
its anchored boats, natives relaxing
beneath umbrellas or standing in the waves.
The day moving lazily toward its close.

If he leaves now, the man thinks,
he might reach his *pousada* by sunset.
And yes, he is praying: praying that he has
smeared sufficient goo on neck and arms

and legs and sandy feet to discourage
the invisible flies that have tortured him
ever since he arrived in heaven.
Always, he thinks, squinting into the sun,

a secret cost. At that instant, three
little girls appear, hopping from the path,
spinning across stone. Six years old?
Eight? Ten? Children are not his specialty.

These three, flowery bikini bottoms,
skinny and brown, topless, are cute
as buttons. He'd like to just put them
in his pocket and take them along with him.

On second thought, probably not a good
idea. Truth is, the man feels slightly uneasy
with the girls' arrival. They crouch and leap
around him, innocent sea creatures.

When one approaches, her high-pitched
voice jabbering a mile a minute a language
he doesn't understand, the man returns
what he hopes is a non-menacing smile.

"Limoney?" she seems to ask him.
"Lemoney limoney?" Idiotically, the man
repeats her, nods as she twirls away.
Then it hits him: the half-full pitcher,

pile of coins on a tray, reused cup.
These monsters are entrepreneurs!
For some reason the man finds this funny,
even reassuring. Sure, he'd take a sip

of that cloudy concoction, why not?,
but has only a single, soggy bill zipped
in his shorts. And nothing's for free.
He thanks the girls, starts down the path.

He hopes he makes it back for that sunset.
Soon follows the moment when the bats
change watch with the swallows,
then a quiet softening of blue to black.

He looks forward to a night of reading.
Of the occasional lonely moment?
It passes. "*Tchau*," the man says, waving.
"Bye-bye," answers one of the creatures.

Feijoada

See, I am fighting for my life in Brazil,
on Ilhabela, in the village of Perequê
on the full terrace of *o restaurante*
Carne de Sol. It is Saturday, so of course
I have boarded bus and arrived,

as I promised the waiter of brutal face
and shortened leg, for the weekly
feijoada, the best on the island, possibly
in all the nation. I have told no one
else of my return, fearfully invited no one,

and when the clay crock heaped with flesh
and black beans arrives at my table,
I know that fear has been justified.
Digging with a large spoon I excavate,
as advertised: chunks of jerked beef,

great slices of sausage and smoked tongue,
fatty hocks falling from the bone.
In addition, a platter mounded with rice
and sautéed kale, topped with broiled
pork chop and wedge of crispy hide.

As precaution, the kale dotted with ham.
At a glance, a rich meal for three men.
It is 1:30 in the afternoon. I clear
my mind of the future, of consequences
and personal costs—a culinary

Zen state for the task ahead—grab salt
and hot pimento sauce, and commence.
Reader, the gruesome details to follow
I will spare you. Suffice to say,
as the next half hour passes minute

by inexorable minute, I am soon sweating
heavily in the cool day. My breathing
grows rapid, shallow. I'm suddenly dizzy.
For a moment, I believe my sight blurs.
In a vision, I see Grandma Brewer,

the pigs' feet and collards she loved
and raised me on. As her kitchen dissolves,
from somewhere above I hear Poe,
a gleeful Montresor hissing in my ear:
Yes, my friend, to the feijoada!

I defeat a bite of beef, raise ritual blade
above the chop, feel removed from time
and space. The pressure to be worthy.
Today I eat for my grandmother!
I eat for literature! I eat for America!

Waxy napkins cling shredded to my hands,
no match for the gelatinous skin.
I am porcine king of shreds and patches.
I attack a piece of sausage that deserves it.
Agua, senhor, agua, I barely choke out

as my torturer limps by. When he returns,
I am forking a hock onto the plate,
a jiggly, defeated thing. Under the waiter's
flat gaze, I assault another hill of rice
with the soupy beans. With surprising

ceremony he twists off the water's cap,
pours a symbolic inch into the small glass,
sets the bottle beside it. He lingers.
I nod my thanks and stab a thick black slab
of tongue, drop it like a mute carcass

beside more kale. I feel delirious, a bit
out of my mind. What will happen next?
A smile lights the man's stony features
as he offers me two big thumbs up.
Is it not all as he promised and more?

Something for Monday

It can't always be
full artillery,
the flame leapt hungry
beyond the pit.
Not every time
the handshake become
a fist through glass,
charred flesh
under the knife, lips
tattooed in blood. The bottle
versus the wall.
The aria
silenced by the curse.
Not always the heat
at your neck,
the night a permanent stain,
on your knees in the dirt
braying like a dog
and none answers.
Sometimes,
the vacant breeze,
the measured gesture.
Careful hand
and steady spoonful,
the wide and unaccusing
sky. A silent voice
controlling
each word that could
and could not
be spoken.

Black Sails

The boats circle the channel on this last race
of the regatta. Bent to the surf, the great black fins
like relics of ruling monsters whose hunger
the entire sea couldn't satisfy. From here, they move

in silence, unique in their unity. I don't know
why you wouldn't answer me, or offer a reason
for the hesitation you knew would dearly cost us.
Our survival in our hands, a chance to seize.

Still you said nothing. I was right, of course.
The door closed, night came. Five thousand miles
away I watch the black sails sharp with wind.
Megalodon, largest shark ever to live, fifty feet in length,

weight of forty-eight tons. Teeth, seven-inch razors.
Can you imagine its instinct at carnage? The awe
of annihilation until no choice remained but to prey
on itself? Gone five million years, or maybe twenty.

Everything is speculation. Good or bad, nothing lasts.
I despise my anger, the mystery of your silence
I can't stop blaming. Our time came and went.
Smell it? It's the sweet scent of blood in the water.

Momentary Interruption

One creature's mutilation becomes another's
play, yet another's interrupted morning.
The blue sky promised sunshine, adventure,

maybe a day worth living, when I noticed
the smudge on the kitchen tile, a wrong thing,
and crouched to look. Gecko the size of a coin,

tail torn away. Likely the little fellow
I had drunkenly cheered on the night before,
zigzagging in starts across wall and ceiling.

The cat José gets his kicks, I was told,
distributing corpses according to whim. Headless,
tailless, or legs ripped off. The tiny toes clung

to my fingertip as if I could save what remained.
I walked to the window, took in the spectacular
view of the coast, the retreating clouds.

The coffeemaker hissed and steamed.
A light touch, a thoughtful nod, then I flicked
the body out over the spiky plants below.

I'm no fan of this killing for sport, of even
such a small life extinguished for pleasure.
But let's not overstate. No one else noticed

or would have given a damn, and I'd forget my
righteousness by the time I'd drunk a second cup.
And as you are surely aware, sashaying

through the room in his lustrous black coat,
José cares not at all whether I disapprove
of his entertainments. José's a fucking cat.

Patron Saint of Aloe Vera

Kingdom *plantae*, of genus *aloe*, species *vera*,
meaning "true," by origin from the Arabian Peninsula,
birthplace of human reverence in the ancient world,
it now grows wild, cultivated, widely coveted.
A stemless plant that spreads by the mystery of offset,

the thick and fleshy leaves serrated by small teeth.
Let us pause our lesson there, on the revelation
of this plant with teeth, sharp and real, each amputated
leaf a treacherous tongue of green. Forget conflicted
trials, the claims of alternative healing drowned

in the babel of science. Shift your studies from ideology
to penitent flesh, red welts whose torturing reality
requires no faith, brooks no forgiveness. Break the body
of the leaf, release the succulence of its power.
Begin with the feet. Paint tender heels, arches itching

beyond night's endurance, the punished ankles.
Slowly up each suffering calf, all that sweet coolness,
that miracle balm, that sublime oozing muck.
Tiny nails gouging the skin, rending each wound
until your blood mixes with the unguent blessing,

pain and pleasure inseparable as meant to be, ecstasy
smeared red down bare legs precluding logic
or reason. Break the plant again. Graze the slick teeth.
My God, you whisper. Eyes closed, head lowered,
you can't stop. This, the mercy you've deserved.

Bonete Beach

If you have the ill luck to find yourself delivered
to the perfection of this remote cove, accessible
to the pilgrim only by mountain pass or

hired skiff, you will learn again the error of desire.
And if, further misfortune, the moon is milky and full,
luminous, stretching tapered shadow across

the dark windows of the beach shacks,
with the entire deserted world at service for your
4:00 a.m. trespass on the divine, that's your problem.

The heaving waves, ceaseless, sparkling like glass,
exhort your grand ambitions and beckon you.
Either that or your life's too puny to notice,

dreams too trivial, fears forgettable. Anyway,
you don't want to get your feet wet. Yet somehow
the moon, wind, waves, black ridge, dark horizon,

are great solace. Mortality? Oblivion? Bring'm on.
Your vows to the fleeting future? As paper-thin
as the message you'll scrawl by candlelight

at a rickety table in your hut—illegible, ludicrous,
abandoned in the morning when the boat arrives
for another terrifying tumble over the sea,

this time destination reality. Meanwhile, soak in
these ineluctable moments of fraught eternity.
Squint hard at the sky. There, the bright North Star?

Go ahead. You know exactly what your wish will be.
No matter that your words drown unheard
beneath the surf's thundering indifference.

You look good, standing out there like you mean it.

5,000 Miles and Counting

until the way back
after it is clear
the remote and painful destination
changed nothing in your life
　　　—Leonard Cohen

Of course, I am the one away.
　　Last night I listened to storm

assault roof, convulse windows.
　　Ticking seconds annoyed,

so I closed the clock in a drawer
　　and the night was timeless.

At the sink, a cool towel pressed
　　to my face, I sensed movement.

The toad who lives in the shower's
　　greenery hunched by the sliding door,

bulging black eyes intent
　　on the violence. I watched with him

as it billowed and raged. That is to say,
　　I miss you, and report this

without irony or fear for reputation.
　　The sky calms. Time resumes

its increments. That is, with luck—
　　and I've been a lucky man, mostly—

in seven days minus hours
    those damn miles, 4,914 to be precise,

will have vanished. Worn out,
    hugging you tight, I'll be home.

And my toad friend? It must fend
    the nights for itself, as we all must.

Sometimes

just a discipline
of stillness
in the body
akin to silence.
No naming
the world's
depredations
or conceding
your own.
Sometimes
just the meaning
of your negotiated
breath, the
tremulous heart,
the hand unfolded
from its fist
and held flat
to calm its uneasy
knowledge.
To neither strive
nor need.
Rather a wordless
prayer,
a humility
akin to belief,
faithful
and hopeless.
Sometimes
no forgiveness
to barter,

no wagered
explanation,
no better choice.
Until the dark
weather passes.

Parrot

The wild world has offered its cares
    so often when I am despondent
        and alone, nearly lost, that I have

come to expect these felicities.
    I wasn't surprised then as I huddled
        on a cold, wet bench

overlooking the channel flint gray
    under cloud, adrift in my futility
        and anger, when the parrot

appeared on the eave of the roof
    and turned an inquisitive eye
        toward me. Plumage a rich and lovely

green. The blunt beak curved
    into a sad smile. No doubt
        of its focus as it settled in for the visit,

or that its soft voice, almost a purring—
    so unlike the hard-edged chatter
        in their darting formations of flight—

was for my benefit. Don't
    misunderstand me: I appreciated
        the effort, this keen attention

to my well-being, and was willing
    to listen. But the darkness had rooted
        in my guts, left my head in a bad,

thankless place. My hands
    craved destruction. So even
        this sweet little bird—the patience

of its clear eye, the cooing rumble
    of its charity—wasn't enough
        to lead me back, and I was afraid.

The Tiny Brown Ants of Brazil

So small that they appear no more
than moving specks, albeit remarkably
quick ones. No sense to be made
of their interest in the shell on your desk,

or your reading glasses, or in the forest
of hairs on your forearm by a sudden
scurrying renegade. You brush it away
without a thought. Let's be honest here:

They are beyond the tipping point
of lives too small to notice or regard.
We needn't consider microbial science
or drag taxonomy into this. Who cares?

Look: You walk twenty feet across the lawn.
It's spring, the grass a silky cool miracle
in your toes! You've caused the holocaust
of a thousand deaths, unloved, unsung,

unavoidable. To cherish one's own life
is to kill, ceaselessly, a moment to moment
carnage, a scale of collateral murder
one can't be bothered to imagine. That's

just how it is. However, if you lean close,
eye just inches from the wall,
you can note distinctly each ginger body—
its segments, the darker head and probing

antennae, a blur of infinitesimal legs
racing from window casing to a cracked
tile on the floor. The manic, ceaseless speed,
the all-consuming and collective drive.

Honestly, they're kind of cute. Who knows?
You resist the impulse to wipe out the clan
with a single tissue, leave them to their
frantic purpose. A blue sky has opened

after days of gloom. So much to celebrate
this morning in the grand parade of life,
your victory march across the big-ass world.
Much more than twenty feet to walk.

A Last Poem Is Always for Lucy

I've seen the photograph, little girl—
    a stockpile of bone, two rawhides,
    and morning treat all clamped
    in your mouth. You are standing

defiantly at the front door, ears raised,
    as if challenging me to return and try
    to take them. *At your peril, buster.*
    Yesterday I walked alone for two hours

up the coast road, a blustery afternoon,
    beaches abandoned, boats tethered
    and rocking. Two bird surprises
    completed my list: a stocky kingfisher

who let me follow for a while,
    then a pair of southern lapwings,
    vain on chopstick legs, backward
    tuft of feather some modish hairstyle.

But you don't care about that, pretty girl,
    nor my anxiety about tomorrow's travels
    by car, ferry, and plane, that I'll need
    a little luck. You having never been,

that is, farther than the 200 miles
    from your rescue, from where I drove us
    home—good God—nearly ten years ago.
    That big day's coming up, and you're

still full of romp and circumstance,
      not to mention questionable attitude
      toward your daddy. I saw the photo.
      You better be ready. Here I come.

Hummingbird, Moonflower

The emerald hummingbird
    flits from bloom to bright bloom
        of the red brush vine

effusive with blossom.
    Hovering, it dips its needle
        in one cup of sweetness

after another,
    with such speed, such trembling
        joy, there hardly

seems time for a sip
    before it stabs at the next,
        and the next, and the one after.

A dizzying display,
    until a larger hummingbird,
        swallow-tailed and dark,

in a squeaking blur
    races the smaller away,
        then perches over a bounty

that could satisfy a hundred
    such thirsts. Here ends the lesson.
        But did I mention

that when I woke
    this morning a note
        had arrived, just a few words

to tell me it was time
    to come home,
        that the moonflower I love,

oddly dormant all summer, would
    bloom tomorrow,
        one of those blowsy,

silky flowers ghostly pale
    in the moonlight, perfect one night,
        that it had waited for me?

Biographical Note

Gaylord Brewer is the author of fifteen previous books of poetry, fiction, criticism, and cookery, including *Country of Ghost* (Red Hen Press, 2015) and *The Poet's Guide to Food, Drink, & Desire* (Stephen F. Austin, 2015). His poems have appeared in *Best American Poetry* and *The Bedford Introduction to Literature*. His many international residencies include Hawthornden Castle (Scotland) and the Global Arts Village (India), and he has taught in Russia, Kenya, England, and the Czech Republic. Brewer was awarded a Tennessee Arts Commission Fellowship in 2009. He is a native of Louisville, Kentucky, and has been a professor at Middle Tennessee State University since 1993.

www.ingramcontent.com/pod-product-compliance
Lightning Source LLC
Chambersburg PA
CBHW021506090426
42739CB00007B/497